Our Pet Rabbits

Written by Suzy Senior

Illustrated by Lucy Barnard

Collins

Meet our rabbits, Clara and Flora.
Flora is my rabbit. She is the plain brown one.

Clara is the one with black spots. She is my sister's rabbit.

They have a smart rabbit house.
The snug shelter keeps out bright sunlight and strong winds.

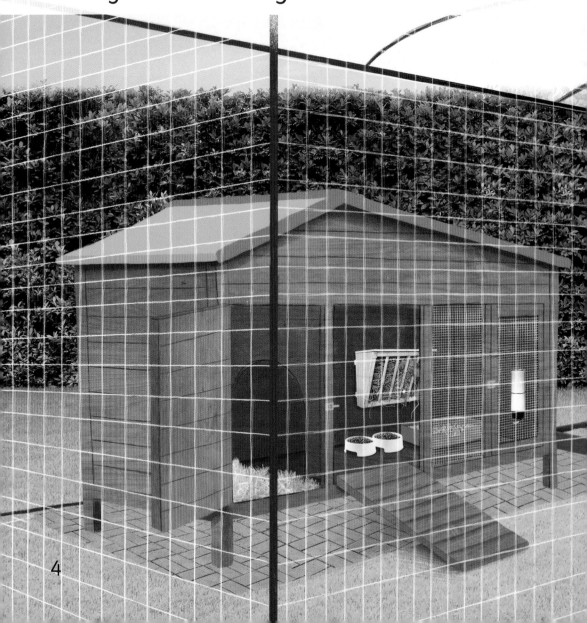

They can roam free in the run. They love hopping and jumping.

run

The rabbit house

rabbit-proof mesh

soft bedding for sleeping

6

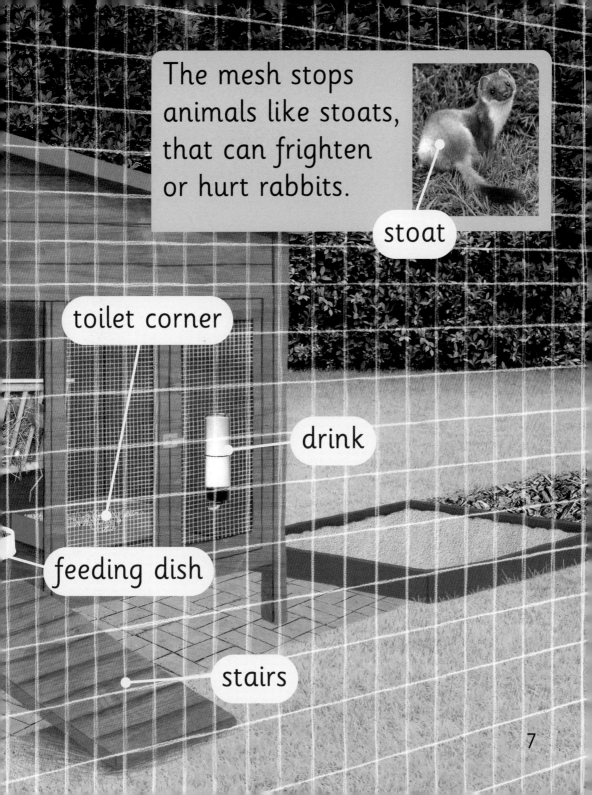

The mesh stops animals like stoats, that can frighten or hurt rabbits.

stoat

toilet corner

drink

feeding dish

stairs

7

Clearing out

We start by sweeping out the spoilt food, and scrubbing the dish.

Next, we scoop out damp bedding and droppings.

Then we put in fresh bedding.

Feeding

Flora and Clara have pellet food.
It comes from the pet shop.

They must have fresh food as well:

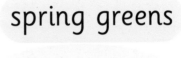

spring greens

herbs, such
as mint

flowers and bits
from some trees

Grooming

Rabbits need brushing.

clippers for trimming nails

soft brush

This keeps Flora and Clara's coats looking smooth and sleek.

grooming mitt

What do pet rabbits need?